Also by Matt and Lisa Jacobson

100 Ways to Love Your Wife

100 Ways to Love Your Husband

100 Words of Affirmation Your Wife Needs to Hear

100 Words of Affirmation Your Husband Needs to Hear

100 Ways to Love Your Daughter

100 WAYS TO LOVE YOUR SON

THE SIMPLE, POWERFUL PATH TO A CLOSE AND LASTING RELATIONSHIP

MATT AND LISA JACOBSON

Revell

a division of Baker Publishing Group
Grand Rapids, Michigan

Published by Revell
a division of Baker Publishing Group
PO Box 6287, Grand Rapids, MI 49516-6287
www.revellbooks.com

Printed in the United States of America

Library of Congress Cataloging-in-Publication Data
Names: Jacobson, Matt, author. | Jacobson, Lisa, author.
Title: 100 ways to love your son : the simple, powerful path to a close and lasting relationship / Matt L. Jacobson and Lisa Jacobson.
Other titles: One hundred ways to love your son
Description: Grand Rapids, Michigan : Revell, a division of Baker Publishing Group, 2020.
Identifiers: LCCN 2019039571 | ISBN 9780800736620 (paperback)
Subjects: LCSH: Parent and child—Religious aspects—Christianity. | Sons. | Child rearing—Religious aspects—Christianity. | Parenting—Religious aspects—Christianity.
Classification: LCC BV4529 .J334 2020 | DDC 248.8/45—dc23
LC record available at https://lccn.loc.gov/2019039571

20 21 22 23 24 25 26   7 6 5 4 3 2 1

INTRODUCTION

How can you find and continue to cultivate a close, loving relationship with your son? Whatever his age, how can you reach and hold on to your son's heart through the years? Perhaps he's young and you already have his heart, but how will you keep it as he grows older? You desire the best for him, but how do you translate that love into a relationship that will endure?

This book is a resource for what to do, what to say, and how to treat sons of all ages. For you to maintain a continuous, growing relationship with your son, he needs to know and experience your love—and that is the reason for this book. Just read one entry per day, reflect on it, and then apply it to your relationship with your son.

Sometimes we need to change what we think. Sometimes we need to change what we say (and how we say it!). And sometimes we need to change what we do. For some parents, it's a minor adjustment. For others, it will be a dramatic reform. But for all parents, it's the journey of loving your son better each day as you are learning to love him well—this kind of intentional love becomes the foundation for a meaningful, trusting relationship that will stand the test of time as he becomes a man.

We have eight awesome children, including four boys ages thirteen to twenty-five. We've walked this parenting journey and are still making it with you. We haven't always done it right and hope you find us to be transparent about our mistakes, but we have close, loving relationships with our sons. Wherever you are on this journey, learning to love your son well is the path to all that's best in your relationship with him today and in the future.

Matt & Lisa Jacobson

MAKE HIM *believe* YOU LIKE TO *be with him.*

My father thought I was an awesome young man. He told everybody this. There was only one problem: he never told me. All the way into my late twenties, I believed my dad didn't really like being with me.

Today we have an excellent relationship (and have had one for many decades), and we've talked all this through. But what a powerful impact it had on me as a young man to believe my dad didn't really like hanging out with me, didn't really enjoy my company.

Many parents think their kids are downright amazing and spend plenty of time talking them up to other people. But for your son to know and then to believe it's true, you're going to have to do more than tell your friends how wonderful you think he is.

The power in a young boy's or man's thinking is what he believes, not what is true. Loving your son requires that you demonstrate, in ways meaningful to him, that you genuinely enjoy being with him.

You could start by verbalizing this truth to your son at a young age. Or even if you're coming at this when your son is a bit older, even if he's a young adult, you can start by saying, "Son, I sure like being with you." Just say those words. So many sons have never heard such affirming words out of their father's mouth. Let your son hear you say them loud and clear.

Another simple, practical way is to invite him to come along with you on one of the many simple outings you might take in the normal course of living. A trip to the feed store or grocery store or pharmacy, or a trip to pick up something in town or to run errands. An invitation is a positive way of saying, "I take joy in being with you." It's a simple thing, but like a lot of simple things in this life, it comes with great power to speak to your son's heart.

Stop WHAT YOU'RE DOING TO *give him a hug*.

I recently asked our fourteen-year-old son what says love to him and figured it would take him a few minutes to come up with an answer. But I was wrong; his response was immediate. "I feel loved when you stop what you're doing, like when you're in the middle of making dinner, and turn around to give me a hug."

So simple. So easy. And yet I didn't always do this. When I was a younger mom, I considered preparing dinner the top priority, and the children could wait. But not anymore. Wouldn't you rather have a slightly burned or delayed meal than miss out on a precious hug from this kid you love to pieces? Same here.

What I didn't realize, however, was that my son would so readily identify that stop-n-hug as what said love to him. It was surprising to hear such a sweet thing coming from this young man who is taller and broader than me now.

Those hugs really do matter. So stop if you're in the middle of something, whether it's making dinner or working or scrolling your newsfeed, and give your son a squeeze. No words are necessary—simply offer a loving hug.

Go ON A BIG *adventure.*

If your son is young, a big adventure might be pitching a tent in the backyard and camping there for the night. If he's a little older, there's nothing like camping in the *bush* . . . Canadian for woods!

I grew up in Tete Jaune Cash, British Columbia, and Dease Lake, near the Yukon border. Mica Mountain (8,711 feet) was outside our front door and loomed over our house like a great giant. I'll never forget my dad taking me up Mica Mountain when I was twelve, far above the timberline, where we spent the night wrapped in our sleeping bags, watching the northern lights sweep back and forth across the endless night sky. We also found fossils of water snails and fish bones!

Another idea is to rent a boat and go exploring. We've rented little crabbing skiffs and caught crabs, boiled them, and had a crab feed. When we lived in Tennessee, we went to Naples, Florida, rented a boat for the day, and went diving for shells. With a little creativity, no matter where you live, there are many possibilities.

Can you think of an exciting adventure your son might enjoy?

Speak A WORD OF *blessing* OVER HIM.

My son had his head down in his studies, so he didn't see me coming. But I made it a point to walk by him and quietly placed my hand on his head, staying silent so as not to interrupt him. But it turned out that way all the same.

He stopped what he was doing and looked up at me warmly and sweetly. Then he said, "You were blessing me, weren't you, Mom." More a statement than a question. *Yes. Yes, I was.* I'd done it so many times that I didn't need to say anything. He already knew.

I usually offer a word of blessing, sometimes only a simple "Bless you, my son," and sometimes I'm more specific. But it's amazing how powerful that small whisper and slight touch can be in your son's life.

Maybe you've never done anything like this before. Honestly, it's really quite easy. All it takes is a few short words as you gently place your hand on his head or shoulder. Then watch how his heart swells and he stands a bit taller.

So, go ahead, give your son a blessing. He longs for it more than he might say or know.

GIVE HIM A *vision* FOR THE *man he is becoming*.

Everything in twenty-first-century culture is about the here and now, about the next five minutes. Tomorrow? Forget about it! That's why parents want their sons to see past the next soccer game, the next get-together with friends, the next fun thing the day holds. That's why parents want their sons to have a vision for who they are becoming as men.

What does this look like in our household? We tell our sons all the time to be mindful that they are building their lives every day. We remind them that the road to their future is paved with today's decisions. We ask, "What kind of man do you want to be when you are in your twenties?"

We ask our sons this because we want them to consider the connection between their decisions today and the life they will have tomorrow. God wants our sons to be men of strength, kindness, and tenderness, with a warlike spirit defending all things that are right, good, and true and taking up the cause of the poor and downtrodden. A future like that requires a perspective that can see beyond the immediate events of their day. You can help give your son that perspective—a vision for the good man he is becoming.

Will he be a man of strong character, virtue, loyalty, courage, kindness? He will be if he is taught to consider others and make decisions that strengthen those character qualities today.

Take THE *time* TO LISTEN.

"What would you say was the best thing I did for you?"

Our son would soon be taking off for college across the country, and I couldn't help asking this question before he left. "In our years together, what mattered most? Between mother and son."

He remained silent, but I could see that he was thoughtfully considering my questions. Eventually, he answered: "You listened to me."

Really? Out of all the things I'd done for him over the past eighteen years, *listening* stood out in his mind? Not the meals. Not the laundry. Not the lessons, nor the lectures. Not even the stories I read aloud.

It's that I'd listened—merely listened while he spilled out his everyday thoughts, his fears, his hopes, and his plans. I heard his little boy's heart and, later on, his dreams.

But at the time, I didn't realize all that patient listening would speak so strongly to him. That my listening would speak love louder than my words.

So, if you have a young, growing son, don't underestimate his need for you, his parent, to simply listen.

Love YOUR *wife.*

One of the most potent ways you can love your son is by the daily, demonstrated love you show your wife. When you love your wife, you are obeying God. He gave direct instruction in Ephesians 5:25 that men should love their wives as Christ loved the church. Reflect on that—it's an amazing standard!

Then you are not only obedient to God but also showing your son how a man is to treat his wife through all the days of married life. Remaining faithful in a world that just doesn't care. You are giving him a vision for the kind of man in marriage that he should be.

You are also giving him a secure foundation from which he can grow and live. The sense of security and peace he will take from the relationship you have in your marriage is as valuable as it is rare in this world.

Have you loved your wife today in demonstrable ways that your son has observed? Show love to your son by loving your wife.

8

ALWAYS *be glad* TO SEE *your son*.

I was typing away on my laptop, working intensely against a writing deadline, when my son walked into the office. Inwardly, I felt the pressure of what I was facing: I didn't have any time to chat right then. Outwardly, I smiled at the young man before me and reminded myself what a blessing it was to have a son around to interrupt me.

He could see I was busy and likely noticed the frantic look in my eyes, so he didn't stay long. But before he turned to leave, he said something that surprised me. "I like it that you're always glad to see me, even if you're unavailable to see me."

What a powerful reminder that it matters—matters a great deal—how we view our children's "interruptions." Is your son in the way of the important stuff, or is he the important stuff? You don't have to drop everything in every circumstance, but it does make a difference if you communicate that you're thrilled to see his dear face, no matter the time or situation.

Let him know you're happy to see him. Always.

Encourage
HIS *gifts.*

I have a friend who is a strong leader and a type A personality. He's got more push than anybody I know.

And then there is his son—quiet, shy, kindhearted, soft, and sensitive. He's more interested in music than in conquering the business world like his dad. And it's all good, because this wise dad understands that he is gifted differently. And it's not just "okay"—it's wonderful!

Consider your son's different gifts. Perhaps you have a world-changer on your hands, or maybe you have someone who is going to work quietly with his hands. These traits are God's gifts to your son and to the world. Whether those gifts are similar to yours or nothing like them, that's the way God made him, and he needs to know you love him as God made him. Encourage his strengths and skills, then watch him blossom in confidence and achievement, the ways God intended, to impact the world.

Show YOUR SON HE IS *loved* FOR *who he is* AND NOT FOR WHAT HE DOES.

I'd finally found my chair and a few quiet moments alone when he knocked on my door. "Hey, Mom, how about I make you a cup of tea and come in and read next to you?" I'd been craving alone time, but you can't say no to an offer like that. Not when he's nearly sixteen and six inches taller than you. So he brought in the tea, and he sat in his chair and I sat in mine. Neither of us said much at all. We just sipped hot Earl Grey and read our books in front of the warm fire, which caused me to consider something.

We live in a world that continually tells us all the things we need to *do* for our kids. So we take them to sports, lessons, parks, places, and Disneyland, running from this thing to that thing without realizing that our kids don't know how to simply *be*. They don't believe they're wonderful just as they are.

And they might not know that because it's not how *you* live. They watch you rushing around, feeling like you're never enough. Trying hard but never quite arriving. So, naturally, that's how they see themselves too. Sobering, isn't it?

But if we want our kids to know they're loved for who they *are* and not for what they *do*, it has to start here—with us. Show your son he is loved for simply being him.

Tell him,
"I WILL PROTECT YOU."

If you follow my Instagram account (@faithfulman), from time to time you'll see an InstaStory about our dog, Jesse. I'm not saying he's the best-trained dog in the world, but he's pretty amazing. Between my dad and me, we've trained him very well. The truth is, I hate untrained dogs, which sounds like a harsh statement, but there's a reason for it. I was bitten badly by a German shepherd when I was a kid, and that experience put a permanent fear in my brain about unpredictable, untrained dogs—especially guard dogs.

One day, my family and I were walking around our neighborhood. Our oldest child was about nine, and out from one of the houses charged a huge Rottweiler, running full speed right at my family. I'm afraid of dogs like that, but I'm also my family's protector. If this dog was going to attack somebody, it needed to be me. I bolted ahead, running as fast as I could directly at the dog.

I had no idea how this was going to end. The fear in my chest grew as the dog and I drew closer together. I'm sure I said, "God, help me" about a thousand times! But when it got about twenty feet from me, that dog turned around and ran the other way. Catching my breath afterward had far more to do with the adrenaline coursing through my body than with being winded.

I'm not saying I'll make the right choice every time, but a man's job is to sacrifice himself to danger to spare his family.

Tell your son you will protect him, and then be prepared to do it, no matter the cost.

LET HIM *experience* THE *joy* OF *serving* YOU.

Every morning our middle son makes French-press coffee and serves it to us with cream and sugar on a wooden tray designated for this very purpose. It's a little something he learned from his dad. And that little something goes a long, long way with me. While I'm not exactly known as a morning person, this loving ritual alone could turn me into one.

People have asked us how we "got him to do this," and we've wondered how to answer. We didn't make him do it, although we did try to model it—this idea of cheerfully serving others. Not only did we model it, but we also allowed our sons to practice giving to us too.

Sometimes as parents, we're so busy serving our kids that we deprive them of the opportunity to experience the joy of helping others, of serving us. But you should see the expression on our son's face when we light up as he walks into the room with that coffee tray. We can't think of a better way to begin our day. Who would have guessed that by blessing us, he would, in turn, be blessed?

Prepare him TO BE A good husband.

Just about every husband learned to be a husband by diving into marriage and blundering along. There are notable exceptions to this, but parents should spend far more time preparing their sons to be good husbands. A world of mistakes, hurt, and devastation would be avoided.

What does it mean to be a good husband? Have you outlined these things for your son? And what's more, have you modeled them for him? Have you thought specifically about the powerful discipleship you can have in your son's heart by the way you conduct yourself as a spouse? And if you're a single mom or dad, you can be successful in this endeavor as well. There are many helpful resources for teaching your son to be thinking in terms of the kind of husband he will be.

Train your son to be thinking about his future as a married man and to consider the quality of husband he desires to be. Start the discussion and continue talking about his future and what it means to be an excellent husband.

OFFER *comfort* IN HIS *time of need.*

I don't know why it stuck with him—this one particular memory—but our oldest son said he remembers the scene like it was yesterday, although I can barely recall the moment myself.

Now an adult, he describes it like this: "I am telling you, there is nothing like a mother's soft hand on a young boy's neck and back. I vividly remember one time when I was sick and burning with fever. I went to the couch and lay down, quite miserable, and now lonely. However, only a minute or two later, my mom was by my side with a cold, wet rag touching my neck and face. A small gesture that still stays with me to this day."

Who would've thought that such a simple attempt at easing his misery would stick with him well into his adult years? I recall wishing I could do more for him, wanting to take away his suffering but feeling helpless that all I could offer was a cool rag and a light touch. I didn't realize that was precisely what his young heart needed at the time.

So be ready to comfort your son when he's sick or hurting or lonely. He'll have fond memories of such times for years to come.

Show HIM HOW TO work hard.

Hard work and good character go together. You can't separate them. God expects your son to know how to work diligently and have a good attitude about it.

When our youngest sons were ages five through nine, winter was coming and four cords of wood needed to be stacked in the shed. A cord of wood is four feet high, four feet wide, and eight feet long. Yes, it was a huge job, but it needed to be done. I knew they could do it, one step at a time. I never touched a single piece of firewood and didn't check on the job until it was done . . . two days later. They did it all. I believed they could do it and then left them to prove it to themselves. Kids are capable of a whole lot!

If you live in the country like we do, there are countless opportunities to teach your son about work. When my boys get tired and want to quit, I tell them that excellent workers work until the job is done, and then I follow up with some positive words about being finished soon. This is love in action.

Maybe you live far from any ranch/farm opportunities, but where you live has no bearing on teaching your son self-respect by his making a meaningful contribution to the family through hard work. The principles are the same whether you live in an apartment in Paris, a mission station in India, near the beach in California, or in a high-rise apartment in New York City. It can be a little tougher in the heart of a city, but the principles don't change and can be applied anywhere.

Take that New York apartment, for example. Someone has to carry the groceries from the store to the tenth floor. Why not commission your son with the job? And be sure to speak encouragingly to him before, during, and after the job is done. Even if your son is only two years old, you can put an orange in a plastic bag and have him carry it and praise him to the skies for his good work.

If we have our heads in the game, it doesn't matter where we live. We can focus the minds of our young men on learning the joy and value of hard work and in the process teach them self-respect, that pillar of good character that is acquired only through genuine accomplishment. Love your son by helping him achieve important things through hard work.

BE WILLING TO *let him comfort* YOU.

Not too long ago, I lost a dear friend to cancer. Although I knew she was in a far, far better place, I grieved deeply.

Her memorial service was on a Sunday, and our family drove me over the mountain pass to attend. Three hours there and three hours back in the same day. Matt asked the boys if they understood why they were coming along. Their answer was honest: they did not. So he explained. "We're going with Mom to show our support. To let her know she's not alone in her grief and we're standing with her." And then they understood.

On the drive there, the boys reached over the front seat to touch my shoulder. During the service, they squeezed my hand and passed me another tissue, and then they hugged me tight all the way out of the church.

To be honest, I'd dreaded that day—saying goodbye to a friend I'd known for so many years. But it ended up being a strangely sweet day. Even in my sadness, I was thankful our sons could see that sometimes the most loving thing you can do is to stay by someone's side.

At times, you might think you want to—or need to—be alone in your sorrow, but don't miss out on the blessing of walking through grief together.

Enjoy him FOR who he is.

Parents often mistakenly want their kids to be who they want them to be rather than who they actually are. Let your son know you enjoy him for who he is, and emphasize he doesn't have to be something else for you to like him, appreciate him, and enjoy him.

He may be unlike you. He may see things differently. He may enjoy different things. He may find different things interesting or funny and feel more intensely about certain things than you do. That's okay. Remind yourself that your son is a unique person—a unique creation of God. And choose to appreciate the ways he is distinct from you. It's important to verbalize this thought to him by saying, "I really enjoy you, son, and who you are as a person. I sure appreciate your terrific personality." These are positive statements about your son, and they remind him that he's great just the way God made him.

There will always be time for correction, discipline, and reminding him that he's off track in various ways, but those moments are more powerful if he first knows, right to the bottom of his heart, that you genuinely appreciate who he is as a person. Many kids grow up believing their parents don't like them very much. What a tragedy. Don't let that happen to your son. Tell him you enjoy the special person he is today!

Don't flip out
WHEN YOUR SON DOES SOMETHING WRONG.

Not too long ago, our twelve-year-old made his best friend cry. I was horrified when I heard about it. Our son said something that deeply hurt his friend's feelings, and there was no taking those words back. I couldn't believe it. How could he have said such a thing? And to this nice young man, of all people?

So my husband sat down to talk it over with our son. At first, he didn't understand what he had done wrong. In his mind, it wasn't that big of a deal and maybe even justified. But his dad patiently and gently pointed out what was hurtful about what he'd said. In time, he saw the implications of his remarks and tears filled his blue eyes. He was genuinely sorry for what he'd done, but it had taken some time for him to get there.

Do you tend to overreact when your son does something wrong or makes a mistake? Remember, your response to your child's mistakes will have a substantial impact on his life from that moment going forward. He needs to know that you're not going to flip out.

Sit down with your son to help him see what he's done wrong and then help him do what he can to make it right.

Pray WITH YOUR SON.

We are quick to pray with our kids when they're toddlers or in the early years that follow, but somehow time causes us to drift away from this practice. Do you pray with your son? From experience, I am confident that just about every parent reading this will answer no. Praying with your son is not very common.

It's time to get back on track (or get on track!). That might be difficult if he's older and you haven't prayed with him for years, but for most of us, praying with your son is as easy as saying, "Hey, son, I'd like to start praying together. Is that something you would join me in doing?"

You don't have to make it some formal ceremony. It can be as simple as spending a few minutes praying in the morning before work or school or at the end of the day before bed. Praying with your son is powerful. And it reminds him of what's essential. There is a God, and we are responsible to Him. He loves us, and He is there to hear our hearts. He wants us to share our failures, thank Him for His gifts, and remember that our lives are His. Show your son you love him by taking the time to pray with him.

Communicate
YOU ARE *confident*
IN HIS *future*.

My son was standing in front of the laundry room sink, washing our free-range chicken eggs, when I walked in to switch out laundry loads.

And that's when these words spontaneously popped out of my mouth: "I believe God has big plans for your life, son." The statement had nothing to do with chicken eggs or laundry or anything else in that little room, other than that young boy standing there.

He stopped washing the eggs and looked up at me with the biggest, most hopeful eyes you've ever seen.

"Really, Mom? Do you really think so?" he asked as if he could hardly believe what I'd said, as if I'd guessed all the doubts and worries that went through his dear, young head.

Except I hadn't guessed them at all. Instead, I'd suddenly had a picture of him as a grown-up man and the many ways God might use his strengths and gifts. So I said it. I said it, and I believed it. And he needed to hear it—more than I could have possibly realized.

And your son needs to hear it too. He needs to know, right down to his toes, that you are confident in his future and all it holds for him.

Hike TOGETHER.

All good parents desire quality time with their kids. But sometimes we try to force the moment, seeking that connection when we haven't truly taken the time to be interested in them as people. Remember the last time you tried to force a conversation with your teenager? Crickets! Wise parents understand that quality time emerges out of quantity time.

This is what makes a hike a great way to connect with your son. Remember, *being* is just as important as talking. So set out on an adventure with the sole purpose of enjoying time and nature together.

APPRECIATE HIS BUILDING *creations* AND SCIENTIFIC *experiments.*

Many moms have asked me how I keep our boys' bedroom clean. I wish I had a good answer, but the truth is, I don't—keep their room clean, that is. I've almost entirely given up, except for the annual "I can't take this anymore" cleaning. We basically run a gauntlet when attempting to walk across their bedroom floor, it is so full of LEGO pieces, airsoft gun parts, and spaceships.

In the beginning, I tried to "organize" their projects and toys, but as you can tell, I no longer even try. Instead, I've decided to focus on the talent and imagination represented in these innovative piles.

Do you want your son to remember a parent who yelled about his messy room or one who was impressed with his creative genius? Do your best to overlook the mess that comes with an inventive, inquiring mind and instead enjoy the creative process and the boy who comes with it.

GET *ice cream* FOR ABSOLUTELY *no reason* AT ALL.

Just about every kid on the planet loves ice cream. And getting ice cream is something you can repeat over and over again, especially throughout the summer.

We were recently at the retirement party of a pastor friend. One of his sons got up and said, "I loved it when Dad would come to my room at 11:30 at night, wake me up, and say, 'Let's go down to the kitchen and get some ice cream!'"

I'm tucking that one away for future use!

Limit THE VIDEO GAMES *and* SCREEN-TIME ENTERTAINMENT.

Sometimes the most loving thing you can do for your son is to put limits on technology and entertainment, although it is perhaps not appreciated at the time. Our oldest son admitted to us that while he might not have been thankful for our "rules," now as an adult he's glad we were willing to do the hard thing back then. He believes it made for a happier and more meaningful childhood, as well as prepared him for a better future in the working world.

Consider how much time your son spends on games and movies, then lovingly put a cap on it that's appropriate for a boy his age. Doing so will help him both now and in the future. After all, spending time on a device does little to encourage a richer, fuller life.

Teach him ABOUT sex AND sexuality.

It's sad to say, but most Christian kids learn about sex from the street, through the internet, or via furtive conversations with people who may or may not have had their best interest at heart.

This is an unnecessary and irresponsible tragedy because the world has nothing to teach Christians about sex, sexuality, or romance. God's Word starts with two naked people in a garden. Remove the euphemistic references to fruit from the Song of Songs, and you've got a solid R rating. No, the world should not be teaching your son about sex. Your church's youth pastor—himself often not yet married and, in many cases, not a mature young man—should not be teaching your son about sex. YouTube videos should not be teaching your son about sex. Risqué movies should not be teaching your son about sex. And his friends should not be teaching him about sex.

Your son should learn about sex from you. He should learn that God loves sex, that God created it for humankind to enjoy, that it's fantastic in the context of what

God created it for, and that there is a great blessing for those who enjoy sex the way God intended.

Shoulder your responsibility, and put away your awkwardness and insecurity. Teach your son about sex before the world has an opportunity to give him a twisted, distorted view of God's beautiful gift to a man and a woman. Love your son by helping him understand the beauty of lovemaking, God's way.

Serve HIM PLENTY OF *delicious food.*

Maybe your boys are different from mine, but I doubt it. Nothing says love to a son quite like a generous portion of his favorite foods. You should see the way our sons' mouths water and their eyes light up when they watch me make my lasagna, for instance.

I don't make it all that often because it's time-consuming and typically requires a special trip to the grocery store. But the effort is undoubtedly worthwhile. They practically beam when I pull out a hot dish of bubbling lasagna from the oven.

Maybe cooking isn't your thing, but are there a few meals you make that your son enjoys? Be willing to take the time and effort to cook one up and then serve it to him with joy. Good food has a particular way of saying love to a growing young boy.

Write HIM a letter.

Spoken words have power in your son's life, but nothing compares to the power of the written word from his own father. When you speak something, time can obscure the influence and meaning of what you said, and the busyness of life can cause it to float away from your memory. But the written word has real staying power.

Some of you might be saying, "But I'm not a writer. I've never written a letter in my life." Don't worry. You're not writing sophisticated literature. A written letter from your heart about what you think of your son, the pride you take in him, the excitement you have for his achievements, and your unconditional love is a powerful way to reinforce everything you've been trying to communicate to him. And chances are, it's a treasure he will tuck away and keep for life.

Laugh
AT HIS
humor.

What do you call a bear with no teeth? *A gummy bear, of course.*

What do you call a cow with no legs? *Ground beef!*

What do you call a cow with two legs? *Lean meat!*

Our boys love making their mom laugh. I don't know why, but they get so tickled with themselves when I find their jokes funny. This also means they'll tell me the same joke over and over again, but that's okay, because it becomes increasingly hilarious the more they tell it. At least to me it does.

So go ahead and laugh at his jokes, his wit, and his one-liners. You'll see there's something mysteriously bonding when you enjoy your son's special sense of humor.

GO ON A *bike ride* TOGETHER.

The thing about great ideas is that they need to be more than plans—you need to actually follow through with them. I'm talking to myself here, because it is easy to let time go by and the pressures of life crowd out all the good moments we intend. So schedule a time to go for that bike ride. And then make it happen.

Think twice
BEFORE YOU LECTURE.

Shaking my head at how my son could mess up such an amazing opportunity, I had to bite my lip to keep from saying anything. I could feel the many wise words bubbling up inside me—all the things he could have done, *should* have done. And I was tempted to drive them home.

Except for one thing.

If he can count on hearing a lecture every time he comes to me about something, he'll stop coming after a while.

I'm not saying that there's never a time to speak up, but there's something to be said for holding your tongue. Just because you or I know exactly what he should do in a given situation doesn't mean we need to share it—especially as he gets older.

Maybe you can use your wisdom to pray for him. It's quite possible that your son will figure out what's right without you ever saying a thing.

So, think twice before starting in on the lecture. Silence can speak louder than you might realize.

TEACH HIM TO
stand up to bullies.

I won't say it's an A-list production, but the made-for-TV series *Hornblower* is excellent for one reality just about every young man faces at some point in his life: bullies. They are a fact of life. Teach your son that the day is coming when somebody will be in his face, probably someone who is a coward, but nevertheless, someone who will try to bully him, shove him around, and brutalize him, or others. If your son is ready for this day, he'll recognize a bully the moment he sees him. Teach your son that men do not give in to bullies, but instead, they stand their ground, do what the situation requires, and defend the weak on whom bullies prey.

ALLOW HIM TO
build forts
INSIDE YOUR HOUSE.

And then sleep in them. Our boys have built countless forts over the years. They've built gigantic blanket forts, pillow forts, and cardboard forts. They even set up a full-sized pop-up tent in the house once. They would spend all day building and then once it was done, they read books, ate snacks, listened to stories, and often slept in there. It was a messy but wonderful enterprise.

So forgo the tidy house and let him build to his heart's content. He's not making a mess, he's making memories you both will enjoy for many years to come.

HELP HIM *understand* THE *easy way out* IS OFTEN *a mistake.*

Our flesh screams at us all the time: "Take the easy way out, do the easy thing." But this is not the way of maturity, and it is not the way of Christian manhood. Help your son realize early in life that choosing the easy path and cutting corners is the way to a diminished future because it is the choice of a diminished soul. The road to the best things in life is paved with hours, days, weeks, months, and years of doing the hard stuff.

Anything worth doing involves difficulty, inconvenience, and hardship. This is simply the way things are. The student who didn't study hard, the student who cut corners, the student who copied other people's work is not the graduate who excels in his chosen field. God calls us to honesty and integrity, and the difficult path to success with God and man requires these things. Men who do not seek the easy way out are men to whom opportunity presents itself.

Welcome THE TRANSITION TO *manhood*.

He was always my cuddler. The first to snuggle and the last to leave. And what mom can resist the joy of holding and loving her little boy? Not me. But then one day, before I was aware of what was happening, he turned to me and said, "Hey, Mom, remember I'm a man now."

He was twelve years old.

Part of me wanted to smile, maybe even laugh. But I could see that this was serious business and I'd somehow lost track of time. Because in so many ways, he was right. Maybe he didn't look like a man just yet, but he was undoubtedly on his way to becoming one. And I didn't want to be the one holding him back by mothering him too much. Or making myself feel better by holding on to him instead of gently pushing him forward.

As moms, we can convince ourselves that when it comes to our sons, manhood is still a long way off. But becoming a man takes some time, and a wise parent shows love by embracing the process.

PLAN A *big trip* TOGETHER— THEN TAKE IT.

If you plan ahead and save a few dollars, it's incredible how far you can go. We're always surprised how much money we can save in a year or two by simply throwing change into a coin jar. This is a fun project for you and your son to do together in anticipation of that big trip. If it's a driving trip, spend some time pulling out maps and poring over them together as you talk about the trip you plan to take. It can also be fun to watch a few YouTube videos of where you'll be headed. Something about planning and then taking a big trip together builds your relationship with your son. It's concentrated time together—just you and him.

FILL YOUR SON'S MIND WITH *inspiring* AND *exciting* STORIES.

Be sure imaginative and adventurous stories play a part in your young son's life. Read the classics aloud to him and encourage him to listen to interesting audiobooks. All our boys have said that these stories have had a significant impact on how they think and what they want to do in life.

One son has listened to the Lord of the Rings trilogy three times—all fifty-two hours, three times over. Now he's old enough to be reading them for himself, and he continues to be enthralled. Another son has listened to the Little Britches series, I don't know how many times. All our boys enjoyed the Green Ember series when they were younger, and they still crack up at *Hank the Cowdog*. Well-written biographies are another fantastic resource to inspire young men to great things.

No matter your son's age, get him hooked on listening to exciting stories, and listen to many together.

SHOW HIM THE *importance* OF *honoring* HIS *parents.*

Many times in a parent's life, even if they have a terrific kid, they will feel dishonored. Your son will do something that will make you feel diminished and disrespected. One responsibility a parent has is to teach their son to respect them.

As a parent, you should want your son to honor you—not so you can maintain a position of authority over him but so he can enjoy the blessings of obedience to God. Honoring you is a responsibility God has placed on him and therefore is not something you are asking him to do. If you are diligent in teaching this truth to your son, those times when he dishonors or disrespects you will be far, far fewer. And your son will be walking in obedience to God.

TELL YOUR SON
how smart
YOU THINK HE IS.

My son was still so young, yet I could see his brain work-ing as he put together the many shapes in this one com-plicated puzzle. He would stare at each empty space for a few seconds until the light went on and then grab just the right piece. I couldn't help but be impressed with his bright mind.

"You're so smart. I love watching the way your mind works," I said as I stood nearby.

He looked up at me with surprise, as if he assumed everyone was a mastermind puzzle solver and nothing was special about what he'd done. But I knew differently and told him so, and he clearly needed to hear it. Your son needs to hear it too.

Maybe he's gifted with numbers or engineering or words or mechanics, but don't leave it up to his teach-ers or friends to tell him so. He wants to know that *you* recognize how smart he is and admire him for it.

BE HIS *parent,* NOT HIS *buddy.*

When your son is a grown adult, your relationship will transition to a respectful adult relationship. And there will be a peer quality to that relationship. But while he is young, your son doesn't need you to be his buddy. He needs you to be his parent. Trying to be your son's buddy is a deeply misguided effort to win his approval. This isn't love, in the best sense of the term. It's an attempt to assuage your guilt or insecurities by seeking your son's acceptance. Even if your intentions are genuine and kind, the endeavor is still misguided and the results are always bad. Your son instinctively knows you are the one to direct, guide, instruct, teach, and protect. When you make him your buddy, you're putting yourself down to his level. He may not be able to articulate it, but he knows instinctively that you're not his peer. You acting like you are is a disorienting and disconcerting experience for him.

Parents are often afraid of losing a relationship with their son and resort to trying to be his friend rather than remaining his parent. When you try to be his buddy, you compromise your guiding voice in his life.

PATIENTLY *answer* HIS *questions.*

"How does the dishwasher clean the dishes?" "Why do you wait for the water to boil before you put the noodles in?" "What's the name of that yellow bird over there?"

While I can only adequately answer one of those questions (that would be the middle one), at the very least I can try to offer some kind of reply. Or perhaps we can look up the answer together. Either way, my attempts to answer his questions tell him I value his curiosity and welcome his numerous queries.

Although it takes time and thought to respond to so many questions, your effort speaks volumes to his heart.

STAY UP LATE
AND *watch*
A *movie* TOGETHER.

It's a simple ask, and he's sure to say yes. "Hey, son, let's stay up late and watch a movie together!" Just add a few drinks, some popcorn, and an additional hour to his usual bedtime, and all of a sudden you've got a sweet memory on your hands. And he'll like the idea so much, he'll likely suggest it for next week too.

Give him A BIGGER-THAN-HIM *job.*

I could feel his beautiful blue eyes studying me, watching me as I worked. He was taking note as I built a fire to offset the early morning chill. His father was out of town and the fireplace is how we like to heat our home, so it fell to me to light a cozy, crackling fire. I was merely doing what needed to be done. But I could sense my son's concern.

"That looks like a man's job to me," he said quietly.

I smiled up at him, not really minding. I'm actually an excellent fire builder, thank you very much, so I kept on with the task. I crumpled paper, piled on small kindling, and then placed the larger logs on top.

And that's when he couldn't stand it any longer.

He stopped me. "That seems like a big job, Mom, so you'd better let me do it."

Those were bold words coming out of a five-year-old's mouth. I hesitated, but his determination made me think I would do well to step aside and let the little man take over. I wasn't sure what to make of him lifting those heavy logs that were nearly half his size, but I admired his confidence to do the hard work.

So build up his confidence and let him try to do that bigger-than-him job.

Respect him
AS A PERSON.

When you have eight kids, one thing is guaranteed—you're going to get several who are very, very different from you!

As parents, we might think our kids' differences are really about right and wrong rather than just about them being "other."

Your way always seems like the right way. Then your son comes along and wants to do things differently, sees things through his own lens, and has his own ideas. It is vital he knows deep in his heart that you respect him as a person. Even if your son is very young, you can begin building respect by endeavoring to understand things from his perspective.

There have been times when I thought, as his dad, I understood why my son was doing something and reprimanded him for it, only to find out that I had misunderstood. I didn't really understand his heart and his reasons. So start seeking to understand how your son thinks about a given situation and honoring the fact that he may see things differently from you. It doesn't mean you don't keep guiding him and offering your perspective, but when he knows he's being heard, you are building into him the confidence that you respect him. And that is one of the most powerful ways you can love and encourage your son.

HELP HIM HAVE A
compassionate heart.

We were driving home over a mountain pass when our daughter with special needs suffered one of her awful seizures. She was sitting in the seat behind us, so I, her mother, couldn't even reach her and wondered what we should do.

But when I looked back, I could see that our teenage son had stretched his long arms around her and was holding her tight.

I'll admit, I used to worry about how having a child with severe special needs would impact the boys. Would they grow up to resent all the extra time and care she requires? Or how she limits what our family can—and can't—do? I couldn't have anticipated what an unexpected blessing she would be—both to us and to them.

Not only does she make us laugh and smile, but each day is a chance to show a little more compassion. A chance for us to slow down and remember what's truly important.

Rather than being resentful, her brothers have developed a tender heart toward her. They cut up her food for her, push her around in her wheelchair, and hold her and pray over her when she's having a seizure. They play with her, tease her, and gently look out for her.

You might have to search outside your immediate family for an opportunity for your son to develop a heart of compassion. But don't underestimate the impact such challenging experiences will have on his life and perspective. Give him the gift of compassion.

TEACH HIM A
new skill.

Gently and patiently teaching your son a new skill is a loving thing to do. And there's nothing like learning a brand-new skill to build confidence in a young man. You can instruct him how to do any of the following:

- pound a nail or drive in a screw
- tie a simple bowline knot (one of the most useful knots ever!)
- chop wood
- grill a hamburger, chicken, or steak
- build a fire
- hang a picture in the house
- wash a car properly

You can teach your son many simple skills, and if you don't know how to do some of them yourself, look it up online. Learn yourself, or some of them you might learn together! And sometimes it's helpful to have a project or two for him to do on his own that will allow him to use his newly learned skill.

LISTEN TO AND *encourage* HIS DREAMS.

Our oldest son went around and recruited as many kids as he could to his "Summer Campaign." At only ten years old, he was a man on a mission. No one was quite certain what might be involved in this campaign, but our son was as sincere as he was persuasive. So he signed up a lot of recruits that summer.

While the details were never clear, he had this dream of fighting for justice in our country and defending the poor and defenseless. It was a big idea for a little guy. We listened carefully while he passionately explained his hopes and dreams for the future.

That boy is now in his twenties, and he smiles when he thinks back on the Summer Campaign of 2004. It might have seemed somewhat pointless back then but less so now that he has his master's degree in national security. But how could we have seen that coming?

Hear your son out as he imagines where he wants to go and what he wants to be. Don't judge whether it's a "good" or "realistic" idea—at least not now. Aspiring young men need a welcoming sounding board. Start listening and let him dream.

TEACH YOUR SON
TO *protect himself*
FROM SEXUAL PREDATORS.

Every good parent wishes their child would never have to face evil at a young age, but sadly, that's not the world we live in.

If your son were facing something evil, you would stand against it and risk everything to protect him, wouldn't you? Your son will experience a lot in life, and you won't always be anywhere nearby. But your words and your teaching can go with him, like armor to protect him in a battle when you are not present.

Teach your son that his body is sacred, and no one has a right to it. Teach him to be on guard and to openly communicate with you about anything that has happened that makes him feel uncomfortable.

MAKE YOUR SON'S *friends* FEEL *at home.*

Somehow our house has become the hangout for our teenage sons and their friends. Maybe it's all the hot dogs, chips, and sodas or the gigantic pots of spaghetti, but they do seem to feel at home around here. They hold airsoft wars out back and watch movies upstairs until long after we're in bed some nights.

And we're glad.

We opened our home because we like the idea of knowing where our boys are and with whom they're hanging out. But we never expected this to be one of the first things our teenage sons would mention when we asked them what made them feel loved. In their eyes, we are loving them when we are enjoying their friends.

So go ahead and invite that bunch of boys over! Cook up a mound of food (or maybe just order pizza), and make them feel at home. Show some friendly love.

Invite him
INTO YOUR WORLD.

Many thirty-something young men these days feel uncomfortable in the company of older men. They feel illegitimate—as if they're imposters and others view them as less than grown men. How does this happen?

The wise parent knows that his son needs to be invited into his company. He needs to be encouraged to step up into the world of adults. It's such a simple thing for a parent to ask a son into his world. When a parent actively takes this simple step, he is communicating manhood to the heart of his son, and he will soon find that his son has a growing sense of confidence in himself and sees himself in a rightful place among other men. Build up your son in this way by making him feel comfortable and settled in your world because you invited him to be a part of it.

SURPRISE YOUR SON WITH A *spontaneous adventure*.

We're not the most spur-of-the-moment family you'll ever meet. I'm too much of a planner and Matt is a pioneer, so we can have a difficult time "throwing it all to the wind" and doing something fun.

But we're catching on that, although it might seem small to us, spontaneous adventures have great meaning to our boys. They love it when we drop everything on a hot summer afternoon and announce we're heading up to the lake for a picnic dinner. We'll inform them that they have thirty minutes to pack up the car, and then it's a mad rush as everyone scrambles to get what they need for an evening by the water.

Sometimes I start to second-guess our decision. I wonder if we're nuts to pull off something like this when we could be eating a sane, civilized meal around our kitchen table at home. But when I see the boys' faces, I catch the excitement of doing something as unexpected as picnicking at the lake on a weeknight.

Perhaps you don't live near a lake, but you could find a pool or skate park or shooting range and see what kind of fun you can enjoy together. Get creative and surprise him!

GIVE HIM *real* *responsibility*.

There's nothing like bestowing responsibility on your son to build him up. We started by having our sons carry mugs with a little bit of coffee in them to the kitchen. It's such a small task but feels rather big to a two- or three-year-old boy.

No matter their age, every son needs to know that someone counts on him. Giving your son responsibility and trusting him with it will tell him that he is an important part of your family. It will let him know that people are relying on him. And it will teach him to think like a responsible young man. When you trust your son with something, you are building him up and giving him confidence that he matters and makes a valuable contribution. Love your son by trusting him with responsibility.

HELP HIM LEARN
good manners
FOR *future success.*

Sometimes I wonder why I bother with teaching our kids manners. It takes so much time, effort, frustration, and endless repeating.

But then I was talking on the phone with my son who was away at college, and here's what he said: "Mom, I never really understood all the fuss about good manners. But you know, now that I'm out in the world, I'm really glad you stuck with it. Because they've come in handy out here. I never realized a simple 'please' and 'thank you' and looking someone straight in the eyes would go so far. They've helped me with my relationships, with getting a job, and just getting around." True story!

Whew. All that trouble—those multiple reminders and promptings—actually paid off! Sometimes I was almost downright nagging, but it helped. And I'm grateful for it. Well, what d'ya know? It's worth the trouble—more than worth it.

So be sure to take the time and the trouble to teach your son his manners. Who knows, he might even thank you for it someday.

TEACH HIM TO HAVE
confidence in
WHAT HE BELIEVES.

For your son to have confidence in what he believes, he first needs to know what he believes. In our household, we start with the Ten Commandments. We teach our kids that these are the things God has laid down as His priorities for how we are to live in this world. And because we teach them that this is God's law, we teach them that what God says, goes. We also teach our kids that God's law supersedes anything humankind says.

In a world without boundaries of any kind, the need for your son to know what the truth is and to have confidence in the truth is more vital than ever. Prepare your son for a world that is going to challenge absolutely everything he believes. Help him anticipate that people will want to oppose and tear down the things he has been taught. Love your son by teaching him to have confidence in what he believes.

GIVE HIM
permission
TO TAKE RISKS.

It was all Matt's idea. He thought it would be fun to rent four-wheelers and take to the sand dunes on the Oregon coast. It was an exciting adventure for our entire family. But a little dangerous too.

Our younger sons wanted to ride their own machines, but it seemed safer to me if they rode in the dune buggy with us. In the end, the boys each got their own quad— less safe but more thrill.

I held my breath the entire time—and said more than a few prayers—as I watched the boys climb the dunes and drop down over the steep, sandy slopes. They had a few minor crashes, but no one was seriously hurt, and the boys had the time of their lives. I have a few more gray hairs, and they have new skills and stories to tell.

Sometimes you need to give your son permission to get out there and try something a little risky.

WORK ON A JOB
together.

There's nothing like a common purpose to bring people together. Whether you're a dad or a mom, you've got the opportunity to work on a job with your son. Only about a gazillion things around the house need doing. So, this week, pick out a project and do it together.

Just remember before you get started, it's not all about efficiency. Getting the job done isn't the point; doing the job together is the point. And it's also not about getting the work done in the least amount of time. Part of a positive experience for your son is that you are encouraging and respectful of his ideas.

Any job will do. If you live in the country, you can chop wood, trim the trees, or till the garden. If you live in the suburbs, you might landscape your yard, wash windows, or clean out the garage. And if you live in the city, you could wash the car together or do any number of other things. The real key is to do the job together and to keep it positive.

And when you're done, be sure to let him know you really enjoyed working with him, and tell him, "Thanks!"

Now, is it absolutely necessary to thank him for helping? No! After all, you've been feeding him for the past how many years? But it is wise because it's another way to say, "I appreciate you," which also says, "I love you."

LET YOUR SON
inside your life.

"How are you doing today, Mom?"

On the surface, it sounded like a basic question, so I started to answer my son with the obligatory "fine." Then I realized he actually meant it. He wanted something deeper, and I needed to give more of me.

Your son doesn't want you to talk only about his life. He wants to hear about yours as well. So let him in on what goes on in your mind, what you're up to, and why you're doing it.

Friends share their lives with one another, and your relationship with your son is a two-way street. He will feel like he's on the "inside," and it will encourage him to share more of his life with you as well.

EMBRACE HIS
masculinity.

Being a boy is normal. Doing boy things is normal. In their excellent books *For Women Only* and *For Men Only*, Jeff and Shaunti Feldhahn clearly outline the scientific proof that boys and girls are anatomically different in regard to their brain structures and functions, not just their physical bodies. They quite literally think differently. In the vast majority of cases, this means boys are going to be generally more assertive and physical, and this is good!

Don't try to soften your son's behavior just because he's acting like a normal young boy. This expression of masculinity needs guidance and correction where necessary, but it's essential for a parent to embrace their son's masculinity and not to view it as some problem that requires treatment or should be altered or stopped altogether.

Masculinity is God's idea, so when you see your son acting in masculine ways, make sure you are embracing and validating who he is as a boy or young man.

This is, fundamentally, about the mindset parents bring to the growth and development of their sons. Have your actions toward your son demonstrated that you value his masculinity? He needs direction. He doesn't need to be changed or fixed. Support him as he goes through the many changes he will experience as he transitions into manhood. That is love in action.

Build up
YOUR SON BY
what you say.

The first time I, Lisa, witnessed the building up of a young son was with a three-year-old boy. His mom and I were deep in conversation, and the poor little guy was quite anxious to show his mom something, but she gently made him wait.

At last, we were finished, and she turned to the dear boy and said, "Josiah, you're patient, and I like that in a man!"

He stood two inches taller. He might have only been three, yet that mom was already building a young man right before my eyes.

Don't wait for the world to inform your son what he is and what he should be. He might be too young to realize it, or he might be older and already being drawn into the current culture, but don't let that stop you. Communicate to your young man—whatever his age—that you have confidence in who he is and who he can become.

Build him up by what you say.

Remember THERE'S A *soft heart* UNDER THAT *tough exterior.*

By now just about everyone has heard the old adage, "People don't care how much you know until they know how much you care."

Your son is no exception to this truth. But sometimes it's easy to forget that under his tough exterior, there's a soft heart. He has feelings even though he may not show them. And he feels them deeply although he may not express himself strongly. Your son is a person, with a heart and feelings that can be deeply wounded with careless words and thoughtless actions. These won't necessarily come from you . . . but they might.

So be mindful of the often unseen but tender places of your son's heart. When you've demonstrated to your son that you genuinely care, it's more likely in moments of vulnerability that he will share his heart with you.

When you forget he has a soft heart, his hard exterior may grow thicker and prevent you access to how he's feeling. He must do this, he thinks, to protect himself.

So be sure to love your son by remembering the soft, vulnerable heart under his tough exterior.

BE THAT *powerful voice* IN HIS LIFE.

I had a sit-down conversation with my son recently. I called him in and said something like this: "Son, you live in a world where everything is about celebrities, star athletes, and powerful CEOs. People will not likely applaud kindness or gentle strength. And they will over-look faithfulness and doing the right thing when no one is looking. But these qualities will set you up for success. True success. They might not make you rich or famous, but they will serve you well."

I then went on to mention several of his strengths that I especially appreciate: his humility, his diligence, and his thoughtfulness. And the tall way he walked out of the room made me so glad I'd done so.

He needs to hear those kinds of words. And he needs reassurance when everything and everyone around him tells him something different—something darker and more discouraging. My son—and your son—needs that strong message more than ever.

We can always look around and hope someone else will tell him. But why not be that person? You are his parent, and you are a powerful voice in his life.

ENCOURAGE HIM TO *respect* THE OPINIONS OF *others.*

Nothing is quite as annoying as a young boy or young man who is so cocksure about everything that he has no time or obligation to consider how others may think or feel or value.

Loving parents who desire to raise kind, respectful young men understand the importance of teaching their son to respect the views of others. As the book of James says, "Let every person be quick to hear, slow to speak" (1:19 ESV).

And when it comes to getting on in the world, the person who follows this advice is competent in life and in leadership. From a purely practical standpoint, you're giving your son a leg up by actively teaching him to respect the opinions of others.

Of course, this doesn't mean he has to agree, and it doesn't mean he has to pretend he agrees. But when he has respectfully heard and considered people's ideas, the esteem in which he will be held by others will only grow.

SPEND PLENTY OF
time together.

Our son was nearly sixteen, a young man with much on his mind and much to do. His days were full with school, friends, sports, dreams, and goals. And on that day, his goal was to get to the bicycle shop. I had to run into town anyway, so I offered to take him.

But when I became pressed for time, his father offered to take him instead. Problem solved. Then imagine my surprise when I watched our son's face fall at the news. He was going to be able to get his bike fixed—didn't he understand that? He explained rather quietly, "But I was looking forward to the time with you, Mom."

Me? His mom? His answer caught me so off guard, I couldn't speak for a second or two. When I finally found my voice, I immediately changed plans—one more time. "I'll take you, son. Let's make that happen. Right now."

I realize now that this wasn't as much about a mountain bike as it was about a young man's heart. A young man who was looking to spend some time with his mom. And a mom who'd been too busy and distracted to see it.

So slow down and recognize that, more than anything, your son wants to spend time with you.

Show him HOW TO BE *resourceful.*

Two phrases are part of our family's culture:

1) Jacobsons never give up.
2) There's always a way to get something done.

We've spoken these messages because we want our kids to view their life circumstances not as a brick wall that is too thick to get through, too high to get over, or too wide to go around but as an opportunity to find the best possible solution. We want them to persevere and to be resourceful.

Oh, I should add one more Jacobson phrase:

3) Go figure it out.

If you do all the thinking for your son, you teach him to come to you whenever he faces a roadblock. You encourage him not to think for himself. But telling him to figure it out on his own expresses three truths to him: you won't always be there, you won't always have the answer, and you won't always be available to solve his problems. Let your son figure it out. Let him go through the frustration of not having a ready answer.

It is only in the crucible of personal struggle that your son can develop resourcefulness. Once he leaves your home, life will not hand him all the solutions he needs. Encourage him not to give up but instead to find the solution for himself.

CONSIDER *splurging* TO DO SOMETHING *extra special.*

When my husband first told me his idea for our family summer vacation, I gulped. We'd never done anything like this, and I knew it was a stretch for our conservative budget. But for years he had wanted to rent a boat and jet skis to play on the lake for an entire day—one crazy and extravagant day for our family staycation.

I was hesitant at first, but he had good instincts and this turned out to be the most amazing, memorable day for our family. It meant the world to our sons, and they still talk about that incredibly fun experience together.

So go ahead and splurge on that special treat. Make a standout memory with your son.

Train HIM TO GET *tough.*

If you tend to freak out every time your son falls or smashes his finger, you're teaching him to be soft instead of tough. If he trips and falls on his face and then, with a glance up at your horrified expression, dissolves into tears, you might not want to be so quick to run to his aid.

Your kids need compassion, but they also need you to understand their circumstances. When your son is young, he is going to pick up on your emotions. Whatever you do—whether you're worried or hysterical or you remain calm, loving, and dignified—he will follow suit. Kids mimic their parents' responses to the things that happen to them.

So teach your son to be strong, to shake off getting shaken up, to shrug his shoulders at that bruise, and not to overreact at the sight of a little blood. Yes, a skinned knee stings a bit, but there's a lot of life to enjoy, so kiss his boo-boo and tell him to go slay a dragon. Loving your son in this way helps him to get tough and keep mistakes and small mishaps in perspective.

Invite YOUR SON TO COME *alongside* YOU IN YOUR *spiritual life*.

Be a quiet example to him and then invite him to follow. For instance, when one of our sons was about eleven, he was invited by his dad to join him for his morning devotions before everyone else woke up. It wasn't something they did together but more of side-by-side time. And somehow this felt like a privilege rather than a burden to our growing man. Not a have-to but a get-to occasion. Two men coming together before their heavenly Father in the early hours.

Your son is waiting for you to invite him to come along. He needs to hear that he's wanted and that you enjoy his company. So ask him to join you—in whatever it is—and enjoy those special moments together.

Take YOUR SON *fishing.*

Don't know how to fish? Then learn together! No matter where you live, you're not far from a fishing opportunity. Whether you're trout fishing in a mountain stream or salmon fishing off the coast or trolling in a lake, it's super exciting when that fishing pole starts to bend! Fishing is one of the most effortless skills to acquire, and many places offer charter fishing trips and training for a lot less money than you'd guess. And it's a great side-by-side activity that says to your son, "I like hanging out with you."

START *conversations* BY *asking* HIM *good questions.*

He is not exactly a big talker, this one son of ours. He is kind, thoughtful, and a man of action. But not necessarily a talker. He's more of the strong, silent type, if you know what I mean.

And as his mom, I don't mind it so much that he doesn't say a whole lot. He doesn't have to be an avid conversationalist, but he does need to be a communicator—not merely for my sake but for the sake of his friendships and future relationships. Because even at the age of twelve, this young man already knew he hoped to marry and become a family man someday. Just like his dad.

And marriage and parenting and friendship . . . they all require communication.

So this silent guy of ours is learning to communicate. We're practicing now with our eye on the future. And you know what I've found? I've discovered it works best if I ask him the questions. He needs me to start the conversation.

Ask your son what's on his mind and in his heart. Ask him lots of real questions. Then listen to what he has to say. Keep the conversation going.

BE PATIENT WITH THE
maturity process.

The next time your son makes a goofy mistake, a wrong choice, or a destructive move, remind yourself of something important: he's a boy in the process of becoming a man, and nobody gets to maturity with a perfect track record.

We're often far too hard on our sons for the very same mistakes (and worse!) we made when we were their age. When we're young, sometimes ideas seem good, but they're not. Time and maturity give us proper perspective.

Love your son by choosing to give him grace, perhaps the grace you were never granted when you were making mistakes. He's on his way to maturity. Be patient and recognize that maturity is a process ... a journey every one of us travels. He needs your wise counsel and instruction, not your condemnation and ridicule. If you are patient, you'll find that he will mature much faster and you will build and deepen your relationship.

ENCOURAGE YOUR SON TO
play outside.

Okay, don't merely encourage him. We'd even say *make* him play outside. He might not be as excited about the idea as you are, but it's the best place for a young man to play and explore as he's growing up. And while he may not thank you now for your little "push," he will later.

Our oldest son put it like this: "I played—the keyword here—*outside* all the time growing up. Hundreds and hundreds of hours. Yes, I had homework and chores, but outside was where I spent my extra time. Those moments are some of the happiest of my life. I have heard 'Go play outside' about a billion times, and 99.99 percent of the time it was from my mother."

Maybe not a billion times, but it's true that he often heard that phrase growing up. It's gratifying to know that while he didn't always appreciate it at the time, he sees now that it was a very loving thing to say to him.

So send some love to your son today and send him outside to play.

VOLUNTEER
together.

The opportunities for volunteering are endless; the needs never stop. There will always be a chance to give a hand somewhere, doing something. So look at the active charities in your area and sign up to volunteer at one of them with your son. You want your son to have a compassionate heart for people who have had a tough go in life, and volunteering can remind him of the blessed life he has in the home where you're raising him. It will also help him see how important it is to love his fellow human beings by giving of himself.

The Bible says pure religion is to look after orphans and widows in their distress (James 1:27). While you might not find such people in your area, it is nevertheless a direct reminder of the priority God places on caring for and looking after the less fortunate.

ENCOURAGE THOSE QUALITIES THAT WILL *bless* HIS *future wife*.

I was minding my own business, sitting happily on the front porch swing, my thoughts pleasantly lost in a good book, when a small missile came hurtling toward me out of nowhere and plopped into my lap. Curious, I gently picked the thing up and, with two fingers, opened it slowly, revealing a handful of brightly colored M&M's—mostly chipped and melted, but M&M's all the same.

Then I saw our son's sweet face pop up from behind the swing. His boyish grin revealed that he was rather pleased with the success of his mission—a loving gift for his mom. The tiny chocolates were from his private stash, and it touched something deep down in my mama soul.

He eagerly explained, "It's chocolate. For you. Because I thought you might like them while you are sitting out here."

He was right, of course. I don't know what I would have liked more at that moment than a pile of melty

M&M's lovingly gathered from his small, sweaty hands. And I thought to myself, *Boy! That's just the kind of thing that will bless his wife someday.*

As mothers, we have an amazing opportunity to teach and encourage those qualities that we know will bless a future wife.

DEMONSTRATE YOUR
loyalty to him.

I happened to be reading a fantastic book on Winston Churchill. And in that book, an incident is recounted when one of Winston's political colleagues tried to have a conversation with him. But this man had made a derogatory remark about Winston Churchill's son, Randolph, who was also in politics at the time.

Churchill turned toward the man and told him that he now considered him an enemy and not to speak to him again. I have to say, I absolutely love this episode in Churchill's life. It's deeply important for your son to know that when the chips are down, your loyalties are settled and you will stand beside him and behind him against all comers. It's one thing to speak of our commitments to each other; it's another entirely to stand with your son when that commitment has a real cost. Certainly, tell your son you are loyal to him. And should life call you to a moment like Churchill encountered, be sure to follow through and demonstrate loyalty by where you stand.

GRAB YOUR SON FOR A *lunch date*.

As a busy, practical mom, I tend to look at running errands or trips into town as merely a job to get done. But I've learned a secret that turns such mundane days into special ones with my son.

If I ask him out for lunch, it's suddenly no longer a chore but a date. I'll usually give him a few restaurant options to pick from and then make a plan. And I'm always astonished by how often we end up talking about things that never seem to come up when we're together at home. He'll bring up details or topics he's never bothered to mention before. I find myself sharing stories from my own childhood that I've not told him before. I don't know why ordering a barbecue beef sandwich at Baldy's Barbecue brings all of this out, but it somehow does.

You should try it. Ask your son if he wants to grab lunch with you and then take him somewhere fun to eat. Don't have an agenda or, ideally, a time constraint. Make it only you and him talking about everyday life over a burger, pizza, or whatever. It might be the best twenty dollars you've invested in something.

So, ask him out to lunch and see where it leads.

TEACH HIM TO
protect himself
FROM PORNOGRAPHY.

In this sin-soaked, sex-saturated world, you can hardly walk down the street without being accosted with sexual material and images of some kind. And then there's the internet—the worst of everything sexual is one click away. It's a danger zone for anyone—men and women—but it's a particularly challenging world for a young man/boy.

In her book *For Women Only*, Shaunti Feldhahn provides clear insight into the scientific literature on the subject of visual stimuli and men. Here's the basic conclusion: men are sexually stimulated visually to a far greater extent than women.

Before we go any further, please ask yourself this question: Am I walking in purity in this matter? You can't attempt to teach your son about protecting himself from porn when you're entrapped yourself.

Teach your son that a woman's body is a beautiful thing to be enjoyed according to God's plan. Teach your son the dignity of women so he will learn to respect them and not see them as objects to disrespect and exploit. Teach him that the day is coming when he will be on his own and have to make a choice between what is right and what is wrong—and the wrong choice leads to destruction and death, just as the Bible says: "The wages of sin is death" (Rom. 6:23 KJV).

When porn flashes in his face—a magazine in a public restroom, a sexy image on his computer, and so on—teach him that by turning away, he is honoring God and all the women in his life.

PURPOSE TO *understand* HIS *personality*.

He's not quite like the others—a quiet introvert in a family of primarily loud extroverts. While everyone else is vying for airtime in our family discussions, this son will stay silent until someone asks his opinion. And even then, we usually have to wait patiently for him to lay out his views.

But something we've learned over the years is that it's worth the wait. He always has something good, something thoughtful (or hilariously witty) going through that head of his. But we have to let him know we want to hear it, or he'll likely keep it to himself. This is part of his personality and essential to know if you're going to understand him.

How about your son? How has God created him? What are his distinct personality traits?

Love him by celebrating his personality.

EMPHASIZE THE IMPORTANCE
OF AN *active lifestyle.*

If you're like me, this one might be a little tough. For the athlete dads out there who are constantly sweating in the gym, mountain biking, MMA fighting, playing tennis, swimming, whatever, this is an easy one for you. But if you're like a lot of the rest of us and don't work out regularly, you may have a hard time encouraging your son to be active. I always want to, I tell myself. I say I'm going to get after it, but somehow the months go by and I let things slide. So I'm writing this for myself as much as for anyone else. Get out there and, like Nike says, just do it!

Life will continuously get in the way and make you feel guilty for taking time out to look after yourself, or at least that's what happens in my head. But being healthy is essential. (As I'm writing this, I'm two weeks into a new health regimen!)

Being in general good health is profitable, and regular exercise is part of that endeavor. If you're lacking motivation, maybe you can watch a video or two with your son about getting in shape. Ask him if he wants to pump some weights with you, for example. He might be reluctant at first, but don't worry. Provide the example by staying after your own fitness program.

It probably wouldn't hurt to lay off the chips and guacamole . . . and that second burger at the barbecue . . . and the third piece of pie . . . and . . . I think I better head out for my morning exercise routine!

DON'T MAKE
impossible demands
ON YOUR SON.

My in-laws rarely interfered with our parenting. Even if they didn't necessarily agree with everything we did, they respected how we parented and gave us room to figure it out.

So it was an unusual request when they asked to sit down to discuss some concerns they had about our approach to our oldest child, who was a toddler at the time. They gently but firmly pointed out that we were being too hard on the little guy. And it was painful to hear.

I guess we were trying to make up for all the way-too-relaxed parents out there by demanding strict obedience from him, at least for his age, and it was too much. Not everyone is thankful for their in-laws' interjecting themselves in their parenting, but I, for one, was truly grateful, because they were right.

Having high expectations of your son is one thing, but demanding more than is possible or appropriate is another. You might want to ask yourself this: Is this reasonable? Could I do this at his age? Am I putting too much pressure on him for where he's really at developmentally?

So, lighten up if you've expected too much from your son.

Tell him,
"YOU ARE A WONDERFUL PERSON."

This is one of those positive statements you need to put in your back pocket and pull out regularly. Nobody gets tired of hearing how wonderful they are. Yet not many kids hear it even once. Love your son by periodically communicating to him that you think he's amazing!

WRITE LITTLE
love notes
FOR HIM.

Words will touch your son's heart. He will long remember the things that were said to him—not only words that were spoken over him but also words that were written for him. And the benefit of the latter is that he can read and reread those words for the rest of his life.

So don't underestimate those short love notes from his own mother. It doesn't take much. A few short lines will suffice if it's from the heart and, most of all, from you. Jot a little note that will cheer him up when he's feeling down, discouraged, or doubting everything around him. Tuck it in his lunch bag. Or place it on top of his dresser. Sneak one in his running shoes. I keep an entire collection of Post-it Notes for this very purpose!

And don't be surprised if he saves them in a box or drawer somewhere and reads them long after he's grown up and long after you're gone. Little notes can go a long way in saying love.

GO TO A PROFESSIONAL
sports event.

It doesn't seem to matter where you live these days, you're not far from an arena where a major sporting event takes place. Even if you live too far away to make it happen in one day, you can go to the game, stay overnight, and come home the next day. Is there a team nearby that your son loves? Why not look into getting a couple of tickets and cheer for the team together!

GUIDE HIM IN BUILDING
solid friendships.

Our second son was on the school basketball team and worked hard to make friends with his teammates. But he was the new player, and they seemed intent on leaving him out, no matter what he tried. We applauded him for his efforts but eventually encouraged him to start looking elsewhere for potential friends.

Then he began reaching out to a few young men who weren't part of the team. They weren't necessarily considered the "cool kids," but better than that, they were the steady, loyal types. The kind of solid guys who become lifelong friends.

Don't be shy about guiding your son in choosing good friends, and help him build strong friendships.

Surround him
WITH STRONG ROLE MODELS.

Sons need their dad and mom. Some have both parents at home, but in a fractured culture or through disease, accident, or a military deployment, many don't have both parents at home. Whether you're single or married, the same truth applies—your growing son needs good role models to look up to.

No set of parents can provide everything their son will need in the course of his coming to manhood. As your son begins to mature and his world expands, he needs the input, exhortation, instruction, and example of other good men. Your son will become the kind of man the men around him are.

Is there someone in your local circle—someone mature, wise, and godly—you can recommend to your son? Or you can be even more proactive. I've mentioned to three men in particular that I respect them deeply and encourage any input they would like to speak into my sons' lives. I tell them they are powerful role models for my sons, and I strongly encourage them to see themselves as having a profound, positive impact on their futures through the influence they wield in their lives.

Demonstrate YOUR *delight* IN YOUR SON.

Although I might be biased as his mom, I'm being perfectly honest when I say every day is a joy with our youngest, a boy, the last of eight. But why were the first few kids "a little challenging" and these last three so "easy"?

The difference wasn't in them. The difference was in *me*.

And I've been thinking a lot about that lately. What was it that changed? Was it that I was a more experienced parent? Yes, but it was more than that. I've come to believe that the secret is *delighting* in our kids. Not just loving them, but liking them too. Not trying to change them—training them, yes, but not forcing them to be someone they're not. And communicating each day that they're a joy to be around.

Joy is powerful, especially when it comes from a parent and is poured over a son.

Let your son know you delight in him. Say it with your eyes. Show it with your touch. Speak it with your words. Love is nice. But love with joy is even better.

INSTRUCT HIM ON
the role of
MONEY.

Even though there are about a zillion ways to teach kids the value of money, many parents teach their children nothing about it. And how tragic is that? Money is not just a fact of life; it's an absolute necessity for getting on, and ahead, in this world.

The Bible has a lot to say about money, and while there are many exceedingly rich men in the Bible and money is never demonized, the love of money is shown to be totally destructive in the life of the person who loves it.

Parents who chase money so they can have the best of everything in life will have a hard time teaching their kids its proper value, because the fact of the matter is that they've already taught them it's an idol and it's well worth spending their lives pursuing. Money is what they should worship.

Money kept in its place is a beautiful thing, while money as an idol sets the worshiper at odds with God.

BE PATIENT WITH YOUR SON'S
energy AND *drive*.

As a toddler, our son would wake up *every* morning at 5:30 a.m. and enthusiastically shout, "What are we doin' today, Mom?!" Cute. But exhausting.

I've never been a morning person. And here I had this high-energy kid. He just had to make the most of every single day. Still does. But I wish I could have seen back then what I can see today.

This boy, with the determined spirit, might have been tiring back when I was a new mom, but God had a plan—and it wasn't to make my life "easy" but to prepare my son for God's purposes. It's important to keep that in mind when you're the parent of a young (or not-so-young) son.

That energy, that drive, that sheer determination—they make all the sense in the world. Although it's a challenge when you're the parent of a lively son, remember God has His reasons for giving him these fantastic—and sometimes fatiguing—qualities.

So patiently smile at that energetic young man of yours. You never know what great things God has planned for him in the days ahead!

LET HIM KNOW
you value
HIS *thoughts.*

Some parents have a tremendously difficult time getting their sons to talk to them and to open up. Does your son know you genuinely value his input? The operative word here is *genuinely*. If your son truly believes you appreciate how he thinks and what he has to say, he's far more likely to open up and engage you in conversation. In addition, when you convince him you do, indeed, value what he has to say, you are building him up and showing him that you respect him. The result is a young man who stands a little taller, who is a little more open, and who has more confidence in himself.

Start praying
TODAY FOR HIS FUTURE WIFE.

I can tell you the exact moment—maybe not the month or the year, but definitely the moment—I began praying for our oldest son's future wife.

I'm sure there must have been a context of some kind, but most of those details have faded. Now all I can remember are the words he said: "I want the kind of wife who would be able to pull an arrow out of my back. That kind of woman."

He was only eleven or twelve years old at the time, so why he would be thinking such thoughts, I'll never know. All I know is that it stopped this mama's heart.

I suddenly found myself full of so many questions, starting with, "Why, son? Why an arrow?" Then, "Why would it be in your back?" and "Who would do such a thing?" and so on.

And finally, "Where in the world do you get these ideas from?" It was our first conversation about his someday wife. But it wouldn't be our last.

You can never start praying for his future wife—arrows or no arrows—too soon and asking God to prepare them for a strong marriage together.

COMMUNICATE
you are pleased
WITH HIM.

Whether it's because of the way we were raised or our life experiences or the things we've learned from other influences, many of us go through life with a vague sense that God is displeased with us, punctuated by moments when He's downright furious. It's common to think of God as some upset dad stomping around with a permanent frown on his face and a flyswatter in his hand, waiting to whack us the moment we step out of line. Many feel as if God can never be pleased.

This is, of course, all completely false. This way of thinking has nothing to do with the God of the Bible. Many of us wind up with this perspective because of parents who seemed never to be pleased, and our first conception of what God is like comes from our experience with our parents. That should strike fear into you and me as we think about the influence we're having on our young sons.

So, teach your son what the Bible says about God and what God thinks of him based on what the Bible says.

PUT CARE INTO
looking after
HIS NEEDS.

My husband was running out the door for a midday meeting, when I suddenly realized he hadn't eaten yet. I stopped him and said to wait a minute so I could quickly throw together a packed lunch for him to take along.

His response was somewhat unexpected. He didn't merely say, "No, thank you." Instead, he appeared to be almost annoyed that I'd suggest such a thing. I was baffled, as it seemed so unlike him.

Later that day, we talked about what had happened in that moment. It took us a while to get there, but then he told me about how growing up, his mom would "slap together" a lunch for him to take to school. Sure, it was food and met his basic needs, but she put little time and barely any care into it. It was just a job, and she did it.

My husband said he knew he should have been grateful for the food to eat, but he used to almost prefer to go without lunch than to have it served like that. He didn't want to be one of her many chores; he longed to feel loved.

So when I think of that little boy's hurting heart and that slapped-together lunch, I'm reminded I want to communicate that I'm happy to put the time and, even more importantly, the care into meeting our sons' needs. They are far more than a job to me.

Celebrate
HIS victories.

Good intentions can really get in the way of celebrating your son's victories. We're all excited for our sons' triumphs, and then the busyness of life comes in and knocks our good intentions out of the way, off the calendar, and before too long, out of our minds. And life goes on.

I'm talking as someone who has allowed this to happen far too often. I can tell you if I had this to do over again with my older kids—remember, I have eight and four are still at home—I would absolutely slow down, take the time to celebrate the victories, and savor those moments.

Purpose to put a signpost, a mile marker, in your son's life by pausing to recognize the rewards he has earned from his hard work and diligent effort. It will remind him how proud you are of him and help sustain him when life tries to diminish his achievements. Love your son by celebrating his many victories through his young years, and beyond.

LET YOUR SON KNOW
it's okay to cry.

Our children can't think of a time when their grandparents weren't a part of our lives and home. Matt's parents lived with us for as long as the kids can remember and were always deeply involved in their lives—from telling stories to playing cards to making pancakes. Grandpa and Grandma J. were always there.

When Grandma finished her long, agonizing journey with Alzheimer's and went home to be with her Savior, many family and friends gathered for her memorial service to say goodbye. One by one, her children and extended family members went up to the podium to share their fondest memories of her.

When it was our oldest son's turn at the podium, he talked about what it was like for Grandma to live with us for over twenty years, ever since he was a little boy. His tears flowed freely the entire time he was talking. Here was our big, strong, weight-lifting son weeping as he spoke of his grandma's life and all she had meant to him.

It's okay for a young man to cry. It's more than okay—it's a fine thing for a son to be able to express his heart and tender emotions.

TEACH YOUR SON
what to look for
IN A WOMAN.

It has been said that there is no accounting for love. How did this person wind up with that person? The Bible itself talks about love, the way of a man with a young woman, as one of the great mysteries.

But this world will bombard your son with the message that the main thing that matters in a wife is physical beauty. Yes, it's important to be attracted to your spouse, but there is so much more to a vibrant, full, loving relationship than a perfect, flawless exterior package.

The world's values are about an inch deep and fifty miles wide—they are shallow. Teach your son to look for a woman who loves God and loves His ways, who has deep character and is diligent in all she does.

In Proverbs 31:30, the Bible says, "Charm is deceitful and beauty is passing, but a woman who fears the LORD, she shall be praised." It's essential that your son value the things that remain, not that which time ensures will never last. Teach him how to choose well.

BE WILLING TO *let go* WHEN THE *time comes.*

Letting go. We know as parents that it's what we're supposed to do, except it's harder than it sounds.

I hear it often from my mom friends. They say they wish their children wouldn't grow up, and they dread the day they have to let them go. And I know that feeling. I tell my husband how much I *miss* those days of making macaroni and cheese, reading stories, and finding the right blankie for naptime. And yet . . .

As fond as I feel about those years, how can I regret what I'm watching now? Seeing them grow up and go out into the world. Doing big and small things for the world and the kingdom of God. It's not necessarily easy for a mom's heart, but it's good and right all the same.

Our sons need us to cheer—and not to hang on.

To speak strong words of confidence—and not to fear for their future.

And they need us to be at peace with the process of their growing up.

Because our sons are not personal gifts for us to grab; they're ours to give to a lost and needy world. So be ready to let go when the time comes. Give your son your blessing and watch what God does.

DON'T LET PUSHBACK
prevent you
FROM SAYING WHAT HE
needs to hear.

As your son moves from child to young man, at some point you are going to experience strong pushback against what you're saying and teaching. But just remember, you're the parent, which means you're the discipler, the teacher, the trainer . . . the one with the responsibility, before God, to raise your son up in all that is right, good, and true.

He lacks experience. He lacks knowledge. However, he may well have the pride of youth and be cocksure about his own position. If he has a forceful personality, confronting him may be more difficult, but all that doesn't change anything. You're still the one God chose to be the parent of this young man. When you're confident your son needs to hear something, don't let the anticipated pushback from him—the snarkiness, the bad attitude, the disrespectful comeback—be a reason you don't follow through.

Be prepared to give your son the tough love he needs. But don't forget the "love" part during your delivery. And don't take the bait when he pushes back. Stay emotionally out of that part of the discussion and press forward with what you know he needs to hear.

FIGHT FOR HIM THROUGH
prayer.

I heard the front door slam and watched our oldest son walk out into the hundreds of acres of open land beyond our property. We don't slam doors in our home, so this was a big deal for our family. He was obviously very upset about something, and I didn't know what to do. When he was little, I could let him cry it out or have him stay in his room until he "got happy" or maybe just hold him tight until he felt better.

But now? He was seventeen years old, and these were no longer our options. I needed to give him space but longed to do so much more than that. What else could I do but go into my bedroom and pray?

I don't think I really understood "wrestling in prayer" until I had a teenage son. He didn't give us much trouble, but he did face intense disappointment, challenges, and temptation. So many times, his dad and I laid awake at night, agonizing in prayer for him. We prayed for protection, strength, and courage for him. We still do.

If your son is young, start praying for him today. And if he's getting older, he needs your prayers now more than ever. Love your son by fighting for him in prayer every day.

TEACH HIM TO
respect himself.

Modeling in parenthood happens whether a parent is a good or a bad example. Whether you are modeling good behavior or bad behavior, good character or bad character, you are shaping them. Kids are all eyes and ears—all the time. What they see and hear informs them about what's acceptable and what's valuable in life.

Even if we model only good 100 percent of the time, we have more to do—we must teach our sons to respect themselves. Self-respect doesn't exist without good character. It is imperative that, as a parent, you teach your son the qualities of good character. A son cannot genuinely respect himself if he is not respectable. And a lazy, bad-mannered, dishonest young man who doesn't know how to respect other people or their property, how to be a good friend, and how to work hard with excellence will never respect himself.

Loving your son is far more than a warm feeling at the thought of him. It involves action—guiding him to become the man he was meant to be.

Is there a character trait you would like to see further developed in your son? Start today by having a conversation about that character trait and then set in motion a plan to work on it.

Remember, modeling the right behavior is good, but it's only a start. Loving your son means teaching him to respect himself.

SHOW HIM YOU'RE
his biggest fan.

Our younger sons have all played basketball for a private Christian school in our town. And being from a small school, the team has had to travel far and wide to play other small schools in our league. And yet I don't think their dad ever missed a single game, even if it meant driving for hours and getting home at 2:00 a.m. That man would move heaven and earth to watch our boys play.

One thing that makes this high level of commitment somewhat ironic is this: Their dad doesn't actually care that much about basketball. What he does care about, however, are his sons.

So you'll see him at every one of their games. You'll see him and you'll hear him, because he's the guy cheering the loudest and with the most enthusiasm. Win or lose. Doesn't matter. Those are his boys and their team out on the court, and he's pulling for them.

So although this dad might not be overly fanatic about basketball, one thing is evident to everyone: he is a true fan when it comes to his sons.

Maybe your son doesn't play sports, but that's not what matters here. What matters is that your son knows without a doubt that you're the president of his fan club. He needs to know you're cheering loudly and enthusiastically for who he is and what he's about in this world.

Leave no doubt that you're his biggest fan.

Tell your son, "I WILL ALWAYS BE THERE FOR YOU."

Whether he's young or getting a little older, life is going to bring some dark moments for your son. Remind him from time to time that no matter where you are, you are available to him and you will come running at a moment's notice.

Remind him you are there for him, you are in his corner, you have his back, he can rely on you. Then when that moment comes, be prepared to drop everything and come to his aid. This might mean taking a call from him at an inopportune time or hopping on a plane and showing up in person.

Whatever it means, make sure you are prepared to follow through on this verbal commitment you've made. Your son will need to call on you at some point in his life. Tell him you are always available and will always be there for him, then follow through on that promise when the call comes in.

ALWAYS WISH HIM
goodnight.

We have long made it our practice to tuck our boys into bed every night. We never made it an extended ritual, but when they were young, they could count on one of us to come into their room to kiss them goodnight. To pray with them, turn out the lights, and leave them with a last note of love.

Our boys are older now, though, and no longer require kisses or lights out. But they still say they like it when we poke our heads in the door and check in before heading to bed—one final connection at the close of the day.

No matter what has gone on in the day, bedtime is a chance to end tenderly and well. Say goodnight to your son and wish him sweet dreams.

Matt Jacobson is the founder of FaithfulMan.com, an online ministry encouraging readers to love God and walk faithfully according to the Word. Matt is cohost (with his wife, Lisa) of *FAITHFUL LIFE*, a weekly podcast focusing on what it means to be a biblical Christian in marriage, parenting, church, and culture.

Matt attended Multnomah University in Oregon and studied philosophy at Trinity Western University in British Columbia. For twenty-five years, Matt has been an executive in the publishing industry. For the past seventeen years, he has been pastor and elder of Cline Falls Bible Fellowship, a thriving community of Christians with a purposeful discipleship focus on marriage, family, and church leadership development. He is a biblical marriage coach and the author of the bestselling book *100 Ways to Love Your Wife*, as well as *100 Words of Affirmation Your Wife Needs to Hear*. For more information, visit FaithfulMan.com.

Lisa Jacobson studied abroad in Paris and Israel and lived in mud huts in Cameroon before marrying Matt and raising and home-educating their eight children in the Pacific Northwest. She is a graduate of Willamette

University and has an MA from Western Seminary. In 2012, Lisa began Club31Women.com, a writing, mentoring, and speaking ministry that has grown into a powerful voice for biblical womanhood. She is also the author of the bestselling books *100 Ways to Love Your Husband* and *100 Words of Affirmation Your Husband Needs to Hear*.

Matt and Lisa cohost the popular *FAITHFUL LIFE* podcast, focusing on what it means to be a biblical Christian in marriage, parenting, church, and culture.

Connect with
Lisa and *Club31Women!*

Club31Women.com

Cohost of *FAITHFUL LIFE* Podcast

@Club31Women

@FaithfulLife

@Club31Women

@Club31Women

Connect with
MATT and **FAITHFUL MAN!**

FaithfulMan.com

Cohost of *FAITHFUL LIFE* Podcast

@FaithfulMan

@FaithfulLife

@FaithfulMan

Hands-on advice
to *LOVE* one another better.

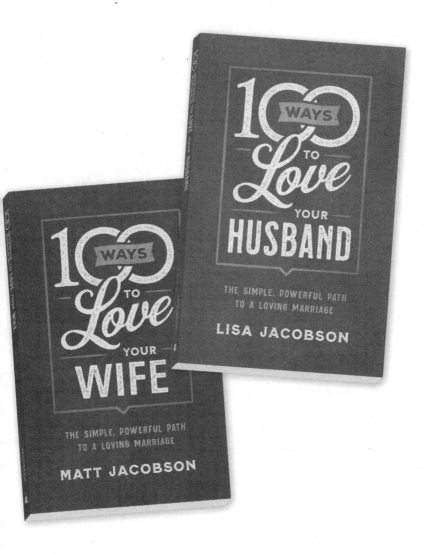

Encouragement to tell your spouse *TODAY*.

MATT & LISA
JACOBSON

Welcome to *FAITHFUL LIFE,* a podcast where we
pursue biblical Christianity on the topics of **marriage**,
parenting, **church**, and **culture**. Biblical teaching,
practical real-life instruction, and *lots of encouragement!*